ιℓ

D0997721

Renewals
01159 293388

THE LONDON BOROUGH
www.bromley.gov.uk www.bromley.gov.uk/libraries
Please return/renew this item
by the last date shown.
Books may also be renewed by
phone and Internet.

ACKNOWLEDGEMENTS

Grateful acknowledgement is made to the editors of the following journals and anthologies, in which versions of these poems originally appeared:

The Poetry Review: "Brixton Revo 2011", "Trinidad Gothic"; *Wasafiri*: "Wild Meat", "Kid/nap"; *Magma*: "Shipbuilding"; *In Their Own Words: Contemporary Poets on Their Poetry*: "Tobago Fruits"; and *Automatic Lighthouse*: "Glenda's Big Decision".

Grateful acknowledgement is also made to the following organisations who commissioned new work:

Victoria and Albert Museum: "A Meditation on *A Portrait of a Trinidadian Woman (The Artist's Servant)*"; Apples and Snakes: "Prayers for Angry Young Men".

For Financial Support: The Arts Council of England for a Time to Write Grant.

For friendship, guidance, support and encouragement:

Nick Makoha, Malika Booker, Suzanne Alleyne, Peter Kahn, Bernardine Evaristo, Imani Wilson, Grace Williams, Dawn Reid, Kevin Martin, Kiki Hitomi, Charlie Dark, Rob Macdonald, Kevin Legendre, Jacob Sam-La Rose, Inua Ellams, Francesca Beard, Piers Faccini, Nii Ayikweyi Parkes, Nathalie Teitler, Anthony Joseph, Breis Ovba, Mc Ty, Lisa Mead, Roba Ofili, Isele Robinson-Cooper, Will Power, Marla Teyolia, Annette Brook, Marc Boothe.

For mentorship and belief in my work:

Kwame Dawes, Bernardine Evaristo; and thank you to Spread The Word's The Complete Works Programme and to Paul Farley for reading, talking through and helping me to shape some of the early poems of the book; and to Jeremy Poynting and all the hardworking people at Peepal Tree Press for believing in the book.

THE BUTTERFLY HOTEL

ROGER ROBINSON

P E E P A L   T R E E

First published in Great Britain in 2013
Peepal Tree Press Ltd
17 King's Avenue
Leeds LS6 1QS
UK

ISBN 13: 9781845232191

Supported using public funding by
ARTS COUNCIL
ENGLAND

For my beautiful wife Nicola

CONTENTS

1

2.

3.

Must I read the *Science Times* to know
that the Monarch's migration
is a fragile journey?

— Ira Cohen

1

PRAYERS FOR ANGRY YOUNG MEN

Prayers for the boys on bmx's swarming the street with switchblade
    stingers,
prayers for the long drips of lifeblood that spray the street like graffiti,
prayers for the stench of curling weed smoke burning away the guilt,
prayers for the young men caught on the wrong road in the wrong
    post code,
prayers for the screw-faced youths who hold on to everything but own
    nothing,
prayers for the buzz of the barber's blade keeping their heads neat
    while their minds are scattered,
prayers for the cocoons of dreams that unravel in sticky threads,
    and for the shy, slender-waisted girls in their beds,
prayers for the hoods pulled up to block out the cold and
    the incessant toll of life,
prayers for the young men ready to rumble and just looking
    for trouble,
prayers for the youths behind bars debating mistakes with time,
prayers for those who bathe tongues in the spoiled fruit of the vine,
prayers for the scars and the wounds of those who lived,
prayers for young pallbearers holding the bodies high,
prayers for those for whom cash is their only belief,
    and for those who steal the fruit when they never plant a seed,
prayers for boys eating neon yellow pizzas and aqua-blue soft drinks,
prayers for those that chew bones while others eat meat,
prayers for the teens watching war on tv and facing a war
    on the streets,
prayers for those who spit anger past dry split lips on the mic,
prayers for boys waiting up for a father's birthday call all night,
prayers for youths with teeth of tombstones who are talking death,
prayers for young men who wear scarred memories on their chests,
prayers for those who spit rhymed poems into mobile phones,
    with Afro-combs stuck in their hair:
to all you angry young men, I offer this prayer.

BRIXTON SUMMER

The Jamaican girls of Brixton
are Rubenesque and ripe.
They stretch the seams
of their primary colour jeans.
Their giant gold-hoop earrings
pull down on their earlobes.
There is dancehall
in the rhythm of their hips
and percussion in their speech.
They wear navel breakers
with shiny, bulging Buddha bellies.
They wait in the queue
texting, only looking up to see
the red glaze of the bus,
as the summer heat
begins to dry the wet sheen
of their pouting lips.

BRIXTON

Electric Avenue's got baby men growing from its pavements,
softness in their face and hardness in their eyes.
They're looking for unmarked cars and business
as the limp-haired heroin addicts are selling me half-price
tickets for the Tube, clothes hanging like loose skin.
Grandmothers press the soft flesh of force-ripe mangoes,
touch the silver crucifixes on their chests,
say a quick prayer and shake their heads over the cost.
Up the street comes a procession of black cars
full of young black men, in black suits.
Someone carved out the heart of their friend;
now it is they who are becoming heartless.
A bespectacled Muslim brother in a white jalabiya
and pitch-black bushy beard sells me vanilla incense
wrapped in silver foil. He offers me a free pamphlet,
tells me to stay black, like I have a choice.
The dancehall queens are licking fried chicken grease
from their long neon-green fingernails in KFC.
Young mc's grab the brim of their new era caps and sip milkshakes
as one of them spits a rhyme in McDonalds.
A young mum in pink Converse is waiting for an empty bus
to get the stroller with the sweaty, sleeping baby on,
the green and gold of a Jamaican flag jingling on her key-ring
as she shuffles from one foot to the other.
The guys at Twin Barbers talk about *Scarface* like it was a documentary.
They stop to survey stolen loot that people bring in from the street:
jeans, shades, t-shirts, cameras. Reggae sleeves look out from a window,
telling people to come in and feel the bass – an hour of the heavy sounds
of downtown Kingston on a mixtape for just ten pounds.
There's new hair on discount in the stores and Afros are back –
but without the revolution. The cockney ticket scalpers
are having a good night and they don't even have to shout.
It's Erykah Badu tonight at the Brixton Academy and African print
headties are out in force. Tonight the mood of Brixton is festive

as the girl in too high heels and a cowboy hat walks with attitude
to the Fridge Bar, watched by the men in black cars cruising slowly.
It's all beauty, it's all hustle, it's love or danger
staring at you at the bus stop.

CHINUA ACHEBE IN BRIXTON

His wheelchair rolls back and forth
in front of Brixton Station, a cheap loudspeaker
distorting his words. I thought he was preaching
about god but he is saying that he is not the *son*
of Africa that he *is* Africa, with his speech
peppered with untranslatable Igbo words.
He is talking of colonisers as locusts
chewing up the resources of the colonised.
Achebe is shouting *Be wary*
of those who take your land
whilst trying to give you their beliefs.
His black beret is tilted on his head
like an commander rallying troops.
His glasses slide down the greasy
bridge of his nose; his wild eyes stare.
If something stands, something else
stands beside it. Do not throw yourself
overboard because someone tells you.
If they can have their god, our gods
can stand beside it.
People talk about toxic waste
being dumped in Africa, but toxic
waste has already been dumped
in your minds. Some of you don't know
how you came to be in Brixton. Hell,
some of you don't know you're African.

BRIXTON REVO 2011

In caps, hoodies and bandannas,
they streamed through Brixton
from small alleys armed with bottles,
bricks and scrap metal, smelling the petrol in the air,
the ashen taste of smoke on their tongues;
they ransacked phone shops, darted in and out
of trainer shops lit by flares of fire.
As thick black smoke billowed
from inside they stood still
for a moment and surveyed the damage:
the crumpled iron shutters,
jagged stalactites of glass;
then, silently, the pack took off,
pumping blood, pumping blood.

BRIXTON FLORA

There are petals of blood
still blooming in the syringe
stuck in the stem of your vein,
a hummingbird sucking
nectar, a stinging bee.
The sharp splinters of ice
in your blood vessels
unthaw; the traffic
and conversation mute;
your head begins to droop.
Your lips are white
encrusted petals,
your skin dry pollen;
your eyes, rose tinted,
roll towards the sun.
They say that once
you were a beautiful flower.

FOUR HAIKUS FOR BRIXTON

Foil
Pieces of crack foil
snowflakes crunching like grit
under the railway arch.

Frost
Up on Brixton Hill
the prostitutes are blowing
frost into their hands.

Soles
Ravers in Brixton
barefeet with black soles, high heels
in their hands, stumbling.

Church
Nigerian women
with their sculptural headties
leave church with heads high.

THE BUDDHA OF BRIXTON MARKET

And as I walked, the walls of Brixton wept blood and devils grew in my yard. I asked one of my customers to pray for me and the holy spirit gripped me by the head and I became heavy with spiritual wisdom. The idea of a holy man brings to mind saffron robes, but I was a humble Jamaican incense seller, with long dreadlocks stuffed neatly in my tam. My chats in the market awakened the sleeper in my listeners' hearts. Spirits barged my dreams and beseeched me to halt at this place. Soon the Bengali butchers crowded round in their lunch hour, then came the barbers, the civil servants, the drug addicts and the drunks. I filled my pockets with amethyst. Too many people at my stall, so I invited them to my flat, but soon the crowd bulged from the door. They hired a hall with a PA. I am not God, I am his instrument. So I spoke and the hall was too small. I did not ask for this. First I abandoned shoes, then meat. Perfumes made my spirit leave my body. They called me teacher, or master. A congregation developed. I must remind you this was not a church. At morning light, my devotees gathered outside the hall, wanting to touch my feet, to be prayed for. My disciples made vows and commitments. People turned up with my picture on t-shirts and bookmarks. I'd hug each devotee after satsang, and they would burst into tears. People from around the world flew into Brixton for the enlightenment of a hug.

2

MONTH ONE

He bought chilli peppers from the market and set his tongue aflame. He spent his last remaining coins on telephone calls home and listened to static. He kept his heater at the glowing-coal setting. His clothing was never right for the weather. Outside he'd breathe the shape of his lungs in mist. His sweat felt like pins and needles. He bought a second-hand leather winter coat that smelled of mothballs and had nothing to do with style. He went to a club with laser lights in the West End. Someone stole his winter coat. He met a woman in the club. She invited him for dinner the next day. She made him a baked potato with grated, melting cheese and baked beans. He'd never had a baked potato before. He waited to see how she ate it. He took a sepia Polaroid of himself next to a red Porsche. He wrote letters back home of pure calligraphic fantasy. He wrote his dreams in the present tense. He kept his suitcase full of clothes in the cupboard to stop it from flying back by itself. He never actually unpacked. He slowed down his speech to be better understood. He was never better understood. He joined a church. He tried to get them to speed up the hymns. They never sped up the hymns. He fell asleep in the sermon. He dreamed about his grandmother and her hair like an Afro cloud. He forgot the name of the street she lived on. The wind in the trees at night sounded like the sea at Maracas Bay. He got a job in a laundry. He felt the warmth of home in the industrial dryers. The windows of washing machines reminded him of planes. Everyone who worked there was from somewhere else. No one talked of home.

THE IMMIGRANT'S LAMENT

His daily ache is memory.
His prayers are to the god of warmth,
with phrases like *the coral reef
of my soul* and *the rumshop
of my conversation*.
When he wakes
he sees a woman's face
in the melting frosts.
By lunch he has lost
his need for seasoning.
Grey is no longer
good or bad.
There's a damp stain
on his wall
the size of his shadow
that watches him as he sleeps.
The snow falls
like pieces of a crumbling sky;
he thinks it turns men
into ghosts.

MONARCH EXODUS

We won't stop till our journey's done.
As throngs of us invade the sky
our countless numbers block the sun.

And when we move, we move as one
and few that fly return alive.
We won't stop till our journey's done.

The time to fly again has come.
We're restless hearts that live in flight
and when we move we move as one.

Most won't get back to where they're from.
We'll rest among the leaves tonight.

The time to fly again has come.

THE IRISHMAN

He didn't board a ship ploughing waves
to Philadelphia, though the potatoes came up
shrunken black, full of fungal canker.
He bribed a ship's captain
taking an empty slave ship to Trinidad.
Looking over the sea, the Atlantic
like a salty boiling broth,
watching the dip and rise of the bow,
he hears the snap of the billowing sails,
the mournful creak of timber caulked
with pitch and prayer.
He thinks about a bar he'll start,
sees the dead who drank
at his alehouse in the faces of
the few mournful passengers.

The watch bell rings out time.
Already the ingrained faecal stench of the deck
makes him plug his nose with mint.
No more the hills of Donegal,
his back turned on the green, green shore,
the sunken eyes of parents with dead
children in their arms behind him now.

He heads to Arima, the east of the island,
to marry my great-grandmother.
What a feat of liberation, what risky genes
flow through my blood? How easily he slips
into this new life. Leaving death
behind, just by a different thought.
How his hair ruffles in the breeze.
How the creaking of the hull
sounds like "new home".

THE PITCH LAKE

Is like a sea, covered with black tarpaulin, soft and firm.
The tour guide tells us where to park our car because
some people came back to find theirs sunk to the roof.
I begin to think what else has sunk here. Occasionally,
the bones of a prehistoric animal or a tree will float up.
This is where Walter Raleigh and his men spread their pox.
While filling their vats to caulk their ships, the smell
of clay and oil pervasive, they raped Ewaipanoma women
and thought of home. While the Englishman was in her
she didn't breathe his air or look into his eyes.
Later, he walked to the centre of the lake
for a bucket of tar to take back to his bobbing ship,
and perhaps he became stuck, this native sex
his last good memory as he sank into soft black pitch,
his struggle making him sink quicker.
The Ewaipanoma girl does not walk out to him,
but sings a song for the protection of his spirit
as he slowly starts the new journey she knew he'd take.

SECOND-HAND BLACK TWEED JACKET

The collar and sleeve are frayed
but the shoulder-fit is perfect,
as if it had been worn for me
by the man whose sweat still lingers
in the armpits, the man who never sewed on
the lost third button. Perhaps his wife
was dead and learning to stitch
lost buttons was too much to bear.
Perhaps this is the suit he wore
when he buried her and the lost button
was a loss compounded, a small thing
but it meant he could no longer fasten
the jacket fully, and so stored it away
in a suitcase with mothballs
whose scents seep into my nose
along with other damaged things.

THE BUTTERFLY WING SUIT

My burlap bags hold wings so light
they weigh hardly anything.
I pierce and drill an eye-hole right
through each of a hundred thousand wings.
I thread each to hessian with fishing line
till I make a suit so colourful, it's bright
enough to hide this dark I hold inside.
In sun, the wings gleam and shine;
each time I step their colours flash,
stir movement in the roosting crows
who gather and then down they dash
like night descending. Their darkness grows.
For winter nests, they pick me bare
till I am ragged in the open air.

SHIPBUILDING

We were always whittling wood
to make ships – a clothes-peg, a lolly stick –
anything that would run the currents
of our drains and gutters.
Shipbuilding constantly on our minds,
we'd look at branches and glue matchsticks
and discuss their seaworthiness.
Soon we realized that our butts
were skinny enough to float down
mossy canals on stormy days.
We became both ship and captain,
floating away, each on his own,
from gutters and drains to the open sea.

ON SEEING THE BUTTERFLY COLLECTION

Seeing their wings pinned
and arranged by genus and size,
it's not so much
their stillness, their colour
or intricate symmetry,
but what they've seen
that intrigues me:
patchworks of fields,
salt-crusted waves,
the grey stone face of cliffs,
the shock of red hibiscus,
the grey-white of clouds.

But now their wings are splayed
and pinned, I can get close enough
to see the dust of their design.
How not to recall the Irish
thought the butterfly the soul
of the dead waiting in purgatory?

Trapped between heaven and earth
neither decomposed nor vibrant,
their patterns like a church mosaic
telling me that they are holy,
their splayed wings
telling me that they have flown.

BLUE MORPHO BUTTERFLY

for the Windrush arrivants

Beneath his Panama hat, his mind held a Blue Morpho,
its aqua wings moving in slow motion in one spot.
He saw the grey buildings and as they put the walkway out,
the butterfly began to fly round the bowl of his skull.
He wiped sweat in his handkerchief and wrung
it out till it poured water, and this water washed
the slicked oil off his hands in factories and wiped soot
off the walls and windows of his first rented room.
The same water baptized his first son's forehead
and chased the rum he'd get from back home.
As he grew old, the butterfly's colour faded to clear sky,
its wings barely moving, but sometimes the taste of sweat
reminded him of the sea-sprayed mists of the deck,
and the homeland where the Blue Morpho can fly.

LETTER TO NICOLA FROM ISTANBUL

From here your smell is chocolates and cream
and CNN keeps me up late watching the news;
I think of how we came together without fanfare,
and you stopped my black necklace of beads from scattering,
and all the countries you couldn't wait to see.
I'm in Istanbul now and I know you'd like it.
Every day I'm looking at things to describe to you:
the morning sunlight on the palaces' gold domes,
the silk parachutes of jellyfish in the clear Bosphorus.
How many nutty brownies did you buy at Leons?
How many bad movies did you watch without me?
CNN is like a bad movie of the entire world
and I wear jackets and ties now, not jewellery,
but I can still hear the tide in your breathing
as you press a gold pin into Turkey on the map.
I can still see the dark river of your hair flowing.

FLOW

This is a story of your heart, its rising and falling tides
of blood pumping through the veined courses of your body
like the tangled rivulets of a delta sluicing into the sea.
Built of platelets and brine, we're held together by skin,
but what of the diffusion of self, that commingling
as the river feeds sea and sea takes river?
Aristotle talks of a single soul inhabiting two bodies,
and we are both water, the river flowing,
again and again unspooling like a grey ribbon of silk,
into the miles and miles of the salt of the Gulf.

CASTILIAN

For Mr Greene

At night under the house,
in the workman's room
I hear a faint Venezuelan mandolin.
I hear his boots on the cement floor,
and I know his hands are clasped
behind his back as he moves
under the bare bulb's yellow light,
around the rusty saw, the plump bags
of cement, his boots shuffling
over a floor strewn with bent silver nails.
Then comes the glissando of a spin.
I know now that his eyes are closed
on the glow of chandeliers
and her dangling earrings.

TO HIS HOMELAND

You put the swagger in my walk
and volume in my speech,
the tidal feeling that tethers me
and floods my thoughts with memories
of ripe mango, my roast breadfruit, my pomerac.
Through the plane windows I watch the clouds
and feel my stress lift as you come in view,
my guava, my coconut water, my red sno-cone.
My passport holds a younger, slimmer me,
creased and cracked, till I renew it
with my red snapper, my stewed chicken, my pelau.
A month in the crumbling house I grew up in
that leaving didn't feel right, though I had to do it,
my tamarind stew, my pepper sauce, my pumpkin.
And when it snows I think of you,
my pommecythere, my sapodilla, my sugar cake.

A MEDITATION ON *PORTRAIT OF*
A TRINIDADIAN WOMAN (THE ARTIST'S SERVANT)
after Alice M. Pashley's batik at the V and A Museum

1.

Her sackcloth dress itches, but she must sit still.
She feels ill from the smell of ash and melting wax.

She is lying down, resting on a bed of fig leaves
and the eaves of sleep are about to fall; she's bored.

She sits up now on the small bench where she shells peas,
taking in the cooling breeze while sifting dirt between her toes.

The sea's night waves are her hair, her skin is wet sand
and her shoulders shrug like she's about to suck her teeth.

Now the fig leaves part for her to see the gate and open road;
she stands and boldly walks away, becoming as small as a wax dot.

2.

Alice Pashley, that's my mother in your picture,
that is the Warai forehead of my aunty,

that is the long lean neck of my sister,
those are the pursed plum lips of my cousin.

They all at one time had to work
for the likes of you, who named them servant.

They all had to grit their teeth to insults
so that their children could eat meat.

They all had to lather your screaming children
and square the edges of your bed sheets.

And because they are not named in your art
I shall name them now: Alicia, Phyllis

Anne, Linda, Florence, Arlene, Monica,
Isele, Mavis, Francine, Rose, Grace, Angela.

3.

I have given you a name and made a life for you:
I shall call you Maria and you live in Belmont.
You did well in school but did not get a scholarship.

You had to stay home and take care of your
four brothers and sisters while your father
looked for piecework on the docks.

You have been cooking, cleaning house
and taking care of babies since you were twelve.
By the time you are twenty-five your family

is grown and you start to look for work
and you sing for tips in the British bar, mostly
jazz standards in the key of colonial.

There's a white woman who stares at you
every night. Her name is Alice. She offers
you twice as much money to clean her house.

So you start cooking and cleaning again,
and sometimes you sit for her to paint
as you hum "Jelly Roll Blues".

One day the bass player from the bar
calls for you at Miss Alice gate,
and you pack and leave without a goodbye.

People say you're a big shot singer
in New York now. Singing in front
of the Louis Armstrong band,

posing with a rose in your hair
for sepia pictures, looking to the sky,
smiling in your sparkling, sequinned dress.

SOLDAT MARTINIQUE BUTTERFLY

You consume poison, to taste
poisonous to others;
birds and lizards keep their distance.

This is your version of safety.
This is what you do to roam
free and slowly amongst the hibiscus.

Because the bitter tonic
does not make you retch,

you can suffer for your freedom
and taunt all of those who cannot.

THE UNDROWNING

His brother's footprints disappear from the sand.
He walks backwards to the hotel and packs his clothes
and heads for the airport, calling his parents on his mobile
and boards the plane back to Trinidad.

Five miles down the coast a bloated body
begins to shrink and dips below the sea where muscles
tauten and eyes open confused and the limbs flail
and stop suddenly, as its expression loses its tension.

Bubbles of air seep into its mouth, and he follows
them up like a fish eating a trail of fishfood.
Then he is pulled upward as if by a line in his back
and flies through the air to land on the edge of the jetty,

where his clothes are dry and he and his friend
wrestle and horse around in drunken play
then he lets go of him and they walk backwards
to the French hotel and pick up the empty bottles of wine.

They spit wine back into bottles till they're full
and pack their suitcases and check out and fly back to London
where they meet me at the airport and I say "no" as they ask
if I'm sure that I don't want to go, that I could still get tickets.

I take their bags and put them in the car and we drive
to my place where they say "time to go", looking at their watches;
they talk about all the girls they're going to get in France,
and we sit and watch cricket whose crowd goes from cheering to silence.

HAIR

Tufts of hair float down to the ground,
swept into heaps, mixed in with dust and dandruff,

it's poured into white plastic bags and tied tight,
sacrificial hair from Indian temples resold in Brixton

hair shops. It gets greased and pulled into ponytails
for the heads of young black working women;

it augments hair covered by black scarves to preserve
the modesty of Muslim women;

it covers the head of my aunt whose hair came off
in chunks in her hand and floated to the ground.

She bought a wig, silver and grey and cut
into a sharp bob; she smiled when she wore it.

TOBAGO FRUITS

There was the pink firm flesh of watermelons,
julie mangoes that smelled like honey,
yellow bananas with black spots,
rare caimats milking at their stems,
rows of ripe yellow pawpaws, and I was in transit
to England with a few hours to kill.
I bought green oranges and sliced pineapple,
salted and peppered in a clear plastic bag.
She offered me some water and asked *Where you from?*
From right here. She shook her head *You're not from here, lately.*
She had her hair tied in a bright white headtie
and her green army shirt was buttoned to the top.
If you're looking for wife I could cook and clean, maybe?
I ent have no children, I doh cause no trouble,
I real quiet an lovin'. I looked at her for a minute
and told her I don't deserve a woman sweet like her.
She gave me a free extra mango and I kissed her cheek;
on the plane I wondered where home was.

3

TRINIDAD GOTHIC

Some of the women in Point Ligoure had already been arrested
for seasoning their husbands' food with a pinch of cement powder.
A stone grew. Grit in an oyster. Chalk in a rooster's gizzard.
Within two weeks they lay dead with a wolf's stone in their stomachs.

The women all had a good reason for this mode of murder
and passed the method on to other women with the same cause.
But alas, too many men of Point Ligoure died at once,
which prompted an investigation, which led to a mass autopsy,

and flaps of stomachs peeled back to find stone after stone,
which led to aunties, grandmothers and girlfriends being led
away in daydresses and handcuffs as other women looked on.
But one clever woman in Point Ligoure found a new way.

You leave an iron out overnight, then before sunrise
you pummel the base of that iron into the soles
of his feet, and you cause an instant untraceable heart attack.
At Point Ligoure, you'll see a dozen irons glinting in the moonlight.

MAZDA MAN

Amongst the greatest local b-boys I saw
at that time, Mazda Man was by far the best,
a breakdancer who'd put shakes in the minds of
any pop-locker in the snare-snap of my generation.
Many a street reputation was destroyed by
a dead-man move, so high and flat, it reeked of madness.
Skinny, with bulging hysterical eyes,
he'd enter the centre writhing and naked
to his waist. Alone he'd leave whole crews
dragging themselves back home broken.
They'd wander aimlessly through the
back-alleys breathless, wondering how
that dark-skinned boy danced his feelings
when they could only do their moves.

WILD MEAT

To know the joy of wild meat,
you see an iguana frozen in your headlights
with its hind leg raised and stuck in midair;
you kill it with a quick blow
of a crowbar; feel its pendulous weight
as you hold it by its tail over an open
flame, then scrape off its skin;
you cut the body into segments;
crunch through its spine
and lop off its head and legs;
you boil it for hours with thyme,
salt and garlic, then serve it
in heavily seasoned tomato stew.
When its meat doesn't yield to your teeth,
and the lump of him sits in your stomach,
your eyes narrow to slits.

AS ALL BOYS DID

For Aaron Bacchus

We knelt and lit
the flame, protected
it from the wind as we dripped
hot wax on the caterpillar.
We looked for the dog,
shaved off all its hair,
called him "rat"
and laughed as he shivered
when we dunked him in a sink
full of ice-cold water.
That summer the game
was to lie in the middle
of the road and to see
who would be last to roll away
from oncoming cars.
We lit fires in the forest hills,
ran blindly down
with flames at our heels,
stole cocoa pods
from the estate trees,
ran and laughed
at the guards' gunshots.
And then there we were,
with our toes curled over the edge
of the roof, daring each other.

HOW TO CATCH A BUTTERFLY

Always come from the side
that does not cast a shadow;
aware of your creeping darkness,
they'll retreat with haste.
Only in summer
are butterflies drunk
enough on sun that you can
approach with fingers
poised like pincers.
Be patient, do not make
sudden moves.
Be as gradual as the change
of seasons. Align your fingers
with their closed wings
and just wait. Do not tremble
or sweat, or let your heartbeat
soar. Keep your breathing
shallow and measured. Then,
when instinct informs you,
close your fingers
at a slow and steady rate.

THE MOURNING GROUND

The waterfall flows
into a clear rock pool
at the mourning ground.
There are ashes and flame-
scorched rock,
two white candles drip-
melted on blue bottles,
an empty calabash bowl
next to wet white robes.
White feathers float in the pool
and there are muddy footprints
on the flat black stone.
They were bare feet.
It looks like dancing.
Was there music?
Now I see blood.
There's some
blood here.

KILLAH

Talked of respect
as something
he craved

in a manner
no different
from any man's.

He made men
into ashes and dust
with his hands

and flashed the sign
of the cross
as he knelt

to pray for
each man he sent
to a stony grave.

He'd say:
If it wasn't them,
it would be me.

KID/NAP

And then there was Uncle Clyde and me in his
car going to buy hops bread when he heard that there
was a wake that night in Siparia for one of his old friends.
Then we were off and Uncle Clyde was soon drinking rum
and helping himself to salt biscuits and corned beef.
We rang my parents and said we would be back tomorrow.

My uncle and I slept in the car, our necks greasy,
the smell of rum suffusing through his pores.
He snored like a sledgehammer.
When he woke we went to Point Fortin
to bathe in the sea; sitting on the sand
he said, *Tonight, we're going to an Indian wedding.*

So we stopped and rang my parents again.
At the wedding I wasn't sure that Uncle Clyde
even knew the bride or groom, but as the music played
he danced like he was the bride's proud father,
making up new dances on the spot,
in his creased clothes and uncombed hair.

We slept on someone's wooden floor that night.
We woke up and they cooked us eggs
and we were on our way to buy mangoes in Princes Town.
With the sweet yellow pulp dripping from his beard
he pointed out the car window: *Roger,*
you see all dem coconut trees, dem ricefields,
all dat cane and dem rivers, all of dat is mine.

TEXTURE

I drive
on black serpentine roads,

the bone-bright full moon
floating ahead,

its face aglow
with acned texture.

This is what moths call god
incarnate.

On journeys they whisper prayers
to its chalk valleys.

TEXACO OIL STORAGE TANKS

(Trinidad Pointe a Pierre 1978)

You silver gods, with viscous black innards,
skin of iron plates and bones of steel rivets,

your Cyclopaean eye is a bright red star.
At each entrance stands an armed, khakied guard;

they check our passes, though we've known them for years,
for though we work here, we don't belong.

A new shift begins, our brown workboots trudge
and the unemployed beg and plead out front

in full view, with burning sun on their shame,
but it's not worse than their child's hunger pains.

Our fingernails are full of tar and dust:
you came for the oil, and left with our blood.

COLLAGE

The parrandero sings with every cell
his four-minute Spanish serenade,
and the shack-shack man
flicks his wrists into the rhythm.
At the baptism, the pastor tries to drown the devil
in the salt water of the sea and looks
to the sky for god to come in.
With a cross in one hand
and a white candle in the other,
all dressed in robes and headscarves,
you'd think this ceremony was Christian,
but just as a drip of blood
falls into a calabash bowl of water
and all turns red,
so a little drip of Africa
has fallen into this ceremony.
The young boy sits
in the river having his head
shaved bald
to honour the death of his father.
The king of the Carnival band
spreads his arms out
like a bird about to fly,
exposing the silver stars
on the draped blue velvet,
and the crowd clears
making room for mas'.
The gentle curve of a finger and thumb
in the wet clay make a tiny deya;
it's beheaded by twine and set aside
for baking – hardened by fire
to hold a burning flame.
Boys walk to school, all with the strap
of their bookbags across their foreheads,

all looking forward to recess
to buy sno-cones covered with guava
syrup and condensed milk.
The fishing boats rest in the shade
of a coconut tree
as the fishermen strip down
to their underwear, taking
the net forty metres from shore
to catch small fish for bait.
The sun's flaring evening rays
are trapped by the deep green of the cove
and sunlight stretches from the pool
to the hotel breakfast room
illuminating redfish and coocoo.
She sits in a burlap-sack hammock
at the front of her shack cleaning rice
before the sun goes down;
as the cicadas start to sing
she goes inside to burn some
garlic to chunkay the dhall.
A white striped lizard poses
on the wall for a picture,
and in the Caroni Swamp
the scarlet fan of an ibis wing
stands out amongst the mangroves.

AREA

For Bert Sampson

With the halos of our angelheaded
Afros, we walk like gunslingers. Hipsters
with thick cardboard dancefloors in our hands,
we'll be burning crews on their own streets.
The troops will trample your territory
like ancient warriors with fresh shelltoes
gleaming under the heavenly stars.
At any crossroad connection,
under streetlights, we challenge
all area cliques, street crews, road gangs
or even the village posse. We are on your turf
dancing under your starry part of the sky.
From the windows of the quaint houses
and shacks you hide in, watch us spin
like dynamos. We mock you with
the heavy machinery of our boom boxes.
We'll dance till you hear the call of battle
and purge your crews from the shadows of night.

How fat they grow on our blood, waiting till dark sets in when they try to get at your head or perhaps a fresh vein of blood at your temple; they're even shooting people in front of the neon lights of Movietown. On every drug corner, boys with twisted caps practice pulling their guns, training for death; every millisecond shaved could save a life of hurt. Mangy dogs with drooping heads and pleading rheumy eyes signal that the sun's too hot and they need water; with heat sapping their pride, even the water from the drain will do. There's a yard of guava, fig and cherry trees with fruit rotting at their feet, a guava split like a cave with rows of ants filing in, bunches of bananas blackening like an ailing diabetic's hand before it's lost. There are the dull tin roofs, some grey, others brown with rust, and each block a quilt of brown grey green and rippling heat. All in thought, we're taking in the breeze through our open doors, shooing away the stray dogs, swatting the flies from our faces. As the sun begins to melt behind our houses, we wonder what to cook. One bandit told me there's no part-time bad boy; when you're in you're in. Even quiet boys from the bottom of my street robbed gas stations from coast to coast in red rubber slippers, with stockings over their heads. Men wait in cars to chop some foreigner into pieces of meat; teenage necks lie broken, limp, the moment of death frozen on their faces. In the forest, men hide from the police; the big man, like King Vulture, waddles next to a carcass, wings crossed behind him. He does not start immediately because death requires contemplation, his face stern and wizened, his eyes shifting from side to side as if there was honour even amongst scavengers – like he knows death. No one is allowed to break skin without his sign and others look on, mumbling under their breath with sideward glances at his vanity and pomp. Then King Vulture raises the v of his white-tipped wing to the sun and sinks his beak into the bloated stinking carcass. With a beard of blood he calls upon his subjects to feast at death's table and they join in. There is no why, there just is, in this bloody month of May, bringing more bullet-riddled bones to be lit by x-rays in Emergency; people who did not know they would be dead today, people with shopping lists for the market and dentist's appointments, whilst the killers, still poor, leave by pirogue or plead for mercy, and the red eyes of the living are looking on, looking on.

SISYPHUS LIMING IN ST JAMES

Sisyphus has been in Trinidad two years now, and he's not going back. Already his favourite bar is Bobby's in St James where he sips Carib beer. The locals have already taken to calling him "Fuss" as a short version of his name, and also because of his anguish over things they think trivial. He tries to hide the keys of heavy drinkers to stop crashes and talks to the prostitutes to try to convince them to change. He is sure that he could learn to be a calypsonian, to the amusement of the bar crowd. They have taken to calling on him when they're drunk enough to hear his latest lyric, which mostly sing of good ways to live. The locals break down in drunken laughter and tell him: *Fuss, calypso is not about preaching, it's about woman, bacchanal and freedom.* Sisyphus tells them he's starting a new form of nation-building calypso, but the rum drinkers are already singing rude old tunes from the past. Sisyphus sips his beer thinking, and nods his head to their drunken tune. *Fuss, everybody just want to have a good time, stop fussing and drink!*

THE CHURCH BY THE HOTEL

After years of complaining
about the moans and slack talk
interrupting their service,

after years of elders cursing
the bare flash of thigh
and cleavage, whispering Sodom,

the church held a vigil
to break the sexual spell
on their lost flock.

They prayed and sang,
their eyes shut tight
behind thick glasses,

the veins on their necks
raised with the power
of their singing.

Working girls within earshot
stopped their clients midflow
and gave them a full refund.

An army of tight t-shirts
thick thighs and face paint
marched to church in silence.

As they crossed its threshold
they all fell to the floor,
kissed the ground and cried.

They cried for every man
they'd had without love.
They cried for hours.

Two weeks later and the girls
changed their lipstick for cocoa butter,
their blouses for starched white shirts.

And they sang hymns in the hot
hot sun just outside the hotel
'til the last working girl came out

weeping, and they cried with her
and told her to raise her voice
in the gospel songs they all knew.

WHERE I'M FROM
After George Ella Lyon

I am from Choppers, chicken coops and cuatros.

I am from the flickering flame of a deya, blue at the wick, luminous, smelling of kerosene.

I am from the tiny engine of a hummingbird revving its wings in front of a frozen splash of red hibiscus.

I am from warm hops bread and rock cake, from Limacol and Senna pods.

I am from bake and shark and callaloo, from tassa and slingshots. I'm from *a little more oil in my lamp* with a small red psalm book and *I'm gonna let it shine.*

I'm from Berec batteries and Sealy Posturepedic mattresses, blue soap and bush tea.

I'm from my grandmother's stroke turning her legs to lead weights, and the slow creep of my aunt's cancer.

I'm from talking with my mother while shelling the peas as she collages the stories of her life which I've lived. Each shell we split, each memory we smile, every pea we value.

THE MONARCH BUTTERFLY

We will gorge ourselves on milkweed,
sip nectar from flowers,
and fly with a belly full of sugary fat
3000 miles at 100 miles a day.
You thought we weren't that tough?
You thought us papery and slight?
We can fly to the spot our grandparents
flew to without ever being there before.
Didn't you know there's a cockpit
of information in our small black heads?
Because you can't explain it,
it can't be possible?
But we are the returning spirits
of loved ones, reminding you
to keep our graves clean.
Think spirit, think miracle
slicing though white mists of clouds;
our dreams fly higher than any butterfly
and at times our love is stronger.

GLENDA'S BIG DECISION

The one man that she'd had
was all she needed to know –
the approving grunts, the kneading
of breasts, hot tongue down her throat,
the shoving of her hips, and the clapping
of skin to jerky rhythms, the sting of sweat
in her eyes, the pulled hair, stretched legs,
stale cigarette breaths, the spit, the spit,
the seasoned smell of hard work
deep in his skin, the yellow
in his eyes looking through her,
like hate like hope like pride,
the wet slobbering on her neck,
the bites, the suck, the mark,
the lift, the twist, the arched back,
then the smell – strong, like bleach –
the wetness slowly snaking its way
down a valley of butt cheeks,
his dead weight pressing down, down.
No, no, this wasn't her type of thing;
the slick of it, the sticky thickness of it.
She only chose him because she knew
his mouth was big and years from now,
he would talk of it as if it were yesterday.
What Glenda wanted was a woman.
She would pay for one of those Venezuelan girls,
all curves and curls and copper skin
from the Metropole Hotel. She had money
from sewing the neighbourhood's clothes
and that's what she wanted. A woman.
Nodding to herself, she rubbed
the sandalwood perfume into her
wrists and took a long slow sniff.

THE BUTTERFLY HOTEL

The phone call at my job said, come quickly.
They thought you might not last till nightfall.
You saw butterflies hovering and floating,
illuminating the dust on top of your tv,

the same butterflies you chased as a girl
in the forests of dried leaves in Couva,
the ones you kept wedged, not squashed,
between the thin blue lines of your copybook.

You'd still enough strength to demand
we should crack a window to free them.
Only I could brave our collective sadness
to tell you that none of us could see them.

A white mask of fear on your face, you asked if they
were not there. *We just can't see them*, I replied.

ABOUT THE AUTHOR

Roger Robinson is a writer and performer who lives between London and Trinidad. He has performed worldwide and is an experienced workshop leader and lecturer on poetry and performance. His one-man shows are: *The Shadow Boxer*; *Letter from My Father's Brother*; and *Prohibition* (all premiered at the British Festival of Visual Theatre at Battersea Arts Centre). He was also chosen by Decibel as one of 50 writers who have influenced the black-British writing canon over the past 50 years. He has received writing commissions from Stratford Theatre Royal East, The National Trust, London Open House and the National Portrait Gallery, LIFT and the Tate.

His workshops have been a part of a shortlist for the Gulbenkian Prize for Museums and Galleries and were also a part of the Webby Award-winning Barbican's *Can I Have A Word*. He has toured extensively with the British Council including Vietnam, Philippines, Argentina, India and the Czech Republic.

His album of spoken folk called *Illclectica* was released on Altered Vibes records in 2004. His album as King Midas Sound called *Waiting For You* is out on Hyperdub records. He has published a book of short fiction, *Adventures in 3D* (2001), two poetry collections, *Suitcase* (2004) and *Suckle*, which won the People's Book Prize in 2009. Between 1998 and 2000, Roger Robinson was programme co-ordinator of Apples and Snakes. He was one of thirty poets chosen for the poets' collection at the National Portrait Gallery.

website: http://www.rogerrobinsononline.com/writing/

twitter: https://twitter.com/rrobinson72

OTHER NEW POETRY FROM PEEPAL TREE

Malika Booker, *Pepperseed*
ISBN: 9781845232115; 84pp.; April 2013; £8.99

Malika Booker's first full collection is bold, transgressive and moving – with a dark womanist humour. It is shaped by the several places she has grown up in and the several she finds home in: London, Grenada and Guyana. This complex sense of rootedness gives her work the capacity to delve into a multiplicity of places, characters, landscapes and languages.

Vahni Capildeo, *Utter*
ISBN: 9781845232139; 78pp.; July 2013; £8.99

In *Utter* the reader is captured by image, sound and beauty of form, and taken into a universe where anything can happen, because there is nothing that can't be imagined. Old boundaries come down: between the past and present, between human and animal, animate and inanimate, between Trinidad, the Caribbean and the global elsewhere, between the experienced world and the world of books.

Raymond Ramcharitar, *Here*
ISBN: 9781845232122; 96pp.; April 2013; £8.99

Here is an epic, formally ambitious, autobiographical poem, in five parts. It addresses the large themes of Caribbean experience: history, migration, education, cultural diversity, myth and domestic love, and sets them in the context of Hindu eschatological myth, locating the holy trinity of Brahma, Shiva and Vishnu in distinctively Caribbean terms.

Kadija Sesay, *Irki*
ISBN: 9781845232085; 90pp.; April 2013; £8.99

The poems in *Irki* tell moving and insightful stories of London and Sierra Leonian experiences which at times convey amusement and affection, at times confusion and sadness. Kadija Sesay writes about the "invisibility" of private fostering, the negotiations of migration and the complexity of home as at once an imagined, remembered and physical place.